Want to know
the world

Volcanoes

Pierre Winters & Margot Senden

Clavis

NEW YORK

It is lovely to walk in the mountains,
to enjoy the healthy country air, and the view of course!
There really is a lot to see. When you think about it, each
mountain is different. This mountain has a tip of snow,
but other mountains...

...look like they are spitting fire!
Wow! This might just be the most spectacular
mountain of them all. It is a volcano. A volcano is
an exceptional mountain. It spits fire and smoke
into the sky and makes a lot of noise!

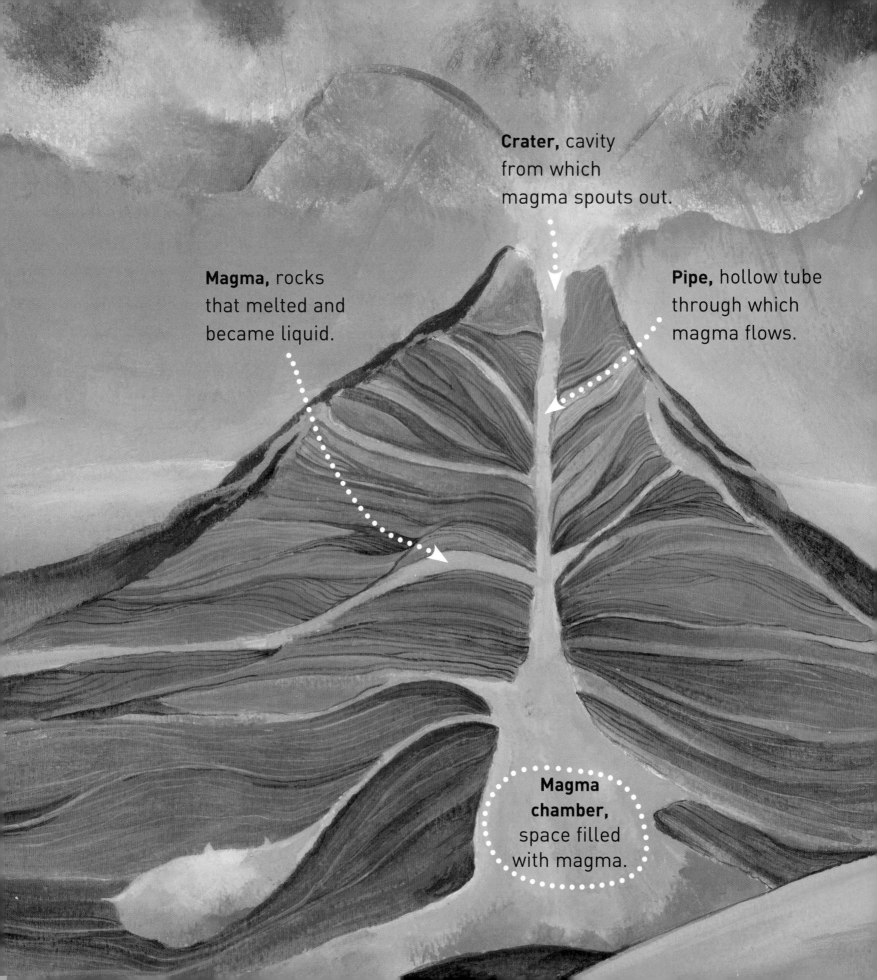

Crater, cavity from which magma spouts out.

Magma, rocks that melted and became liquid.

Pipe, hollow tube through which magma flows.

Magma chamber, space filled with magma.

What are volcanoes?

The earth is a giant ball. Inside that ball it is so hot that even rocks melt. It's red-hot!
Fortunately there is a kind of covering around that fiery porridge: the earth's crust.
Usually the earth's crust is nice and thick, so you do not notice the bubbling inside.
But in some places the crust is thinner or there are cracks in the crust.
In these spots the fiery porridge sometimes breaks out!
And that is exactly what a volcano is: a place
where the fiery porridge escapes.

Did you know
the word "volcano" comes
from the Roman god Vulcan?
He was the god of fire.

How does a volcano erupt?

A volcano does not erupt suddenly. It happens in steps.

1 Here everything is OK. There is boiling magma inside the volcano, but it cannot escape because the pipe is filled with rocks. These rocks form a kind of plug.

2 More and more magma builds inside the volcano. The magma chambers get fuller and fuller. There's too much magma to fit. That's why the magma begins to push against the sides and against the plug. If you look carefully you can see steam escaping in some places.

3 Even more magma has built. That magma now pushes against the inside of the volcano so hard that the plug flies out with a big bang. With huge force the molten rock comes shooting out. This is a volcanic eruption.

Magma is pushing up against the underside of the earth's crust.

How do volcanoes come into being?

Volcanic ash, little pieces of rock, minerals and dust that burst out during an eruption.

Fissure, a crack in the earth's crust or in the volcano. This is how the lava escapes.

The earth's crust consists of separate pieces just like an enormous jigsaw puzzle. The pieces of the earth's crust are always moving. They float towards one another or away from one another. This happens so slowly that people do not usually notice it happening. Sometimes two pieces bump into each other. When this happens rocks and boulders get pushed upwards. This can create mountains. Or volcanoes. Because if two pieces of the earth's crust rub over each other, they push on the magma below.

Geyser, sometimes there is water just above the magma. The heat of the magma causes the water to boil and expand until it bursts up in a spout. It's a kind of volcano, but with water instead of lava.

Did you know the pieces of the earth's crust only move a couple of inches each year? That's why it takes thousands of years for a mountain to become really big.

And when they push hard enough, the magma has to escape. And you know what happens next! This is the reason that most volcanoes lie at the edges of the puzzle pieces.

Under water!

It might sound
a bit strange, but most
volcanoes are under water.
That's a good thing, because
that way they do not bother
humans. These volcanoes work
the same way as regular volcanoes,
they are just submerged. If a volcano
erupts under water, the water above it
starts to bubble and boil. This can create
really big waves. When a volcano erupts, the
lava often ends up right on top of the volcano.
It cools down and solidifies. That way the volcano
becomes a little bit bigger. If this happens many times
to an underwater volcano, it can grow so big that it sticks out
above the water. That's how new islands come into being.

Did you know "eruption" is a big word for an outburst?

Did you know
the American volcano Mount Saint Helens was dormant for over a hundred years? Nobody thought it would ever erupt again, but it went and did it anyway!

Famous volcanoes

Mount Saint Helens in Washington state is famous because in 1980 it erupted with such force that it actually became smaller. Here you can see what it looked like first: proud and big. It was a dormant volcano ("dormant" means "sleeping"). On the other side of this page you can see what Mount Saint Helens looks like now.

Where are most volcanoes found?

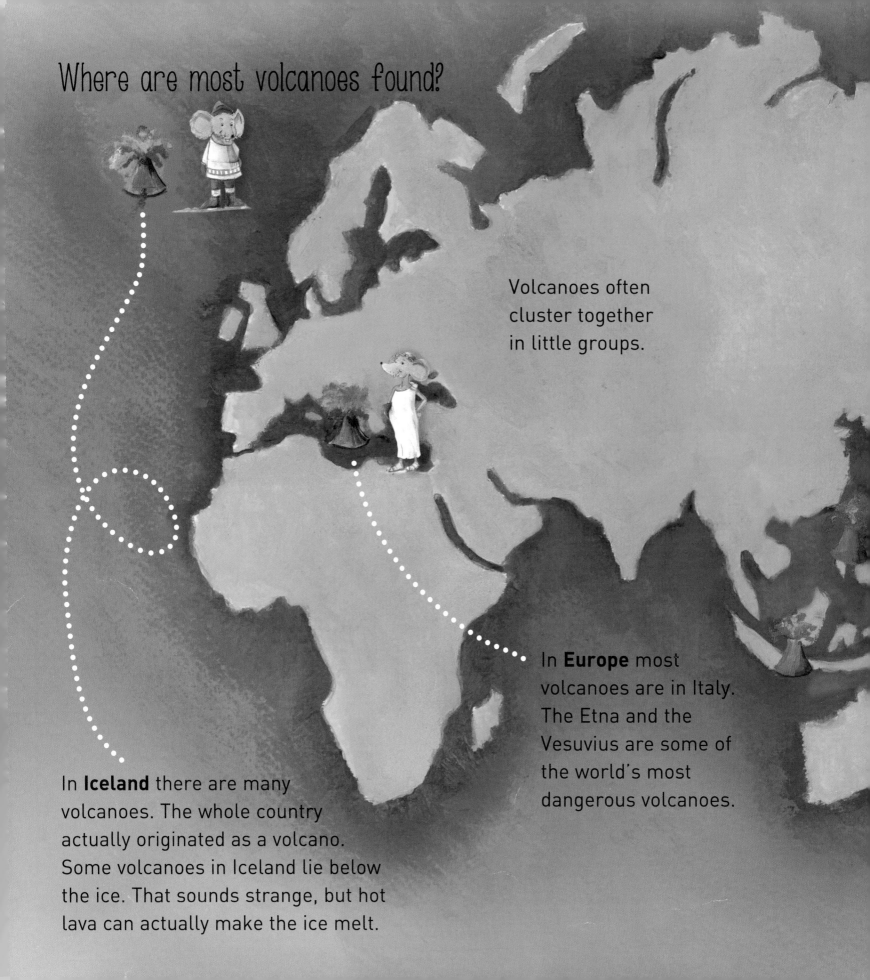

Volcanoes often cluster together in little groups.

In **Europe** most volcanoes are in Italy. The Etna and the Vesuvius are some of the world's most dangerous volcanoes.

In **Iceland** there are many volcanoes. The whole country actually originated as a volcano. Some volcanoes in Iceland lie below the ice. That sounds strange, but hot lava can actually make the ice melt.

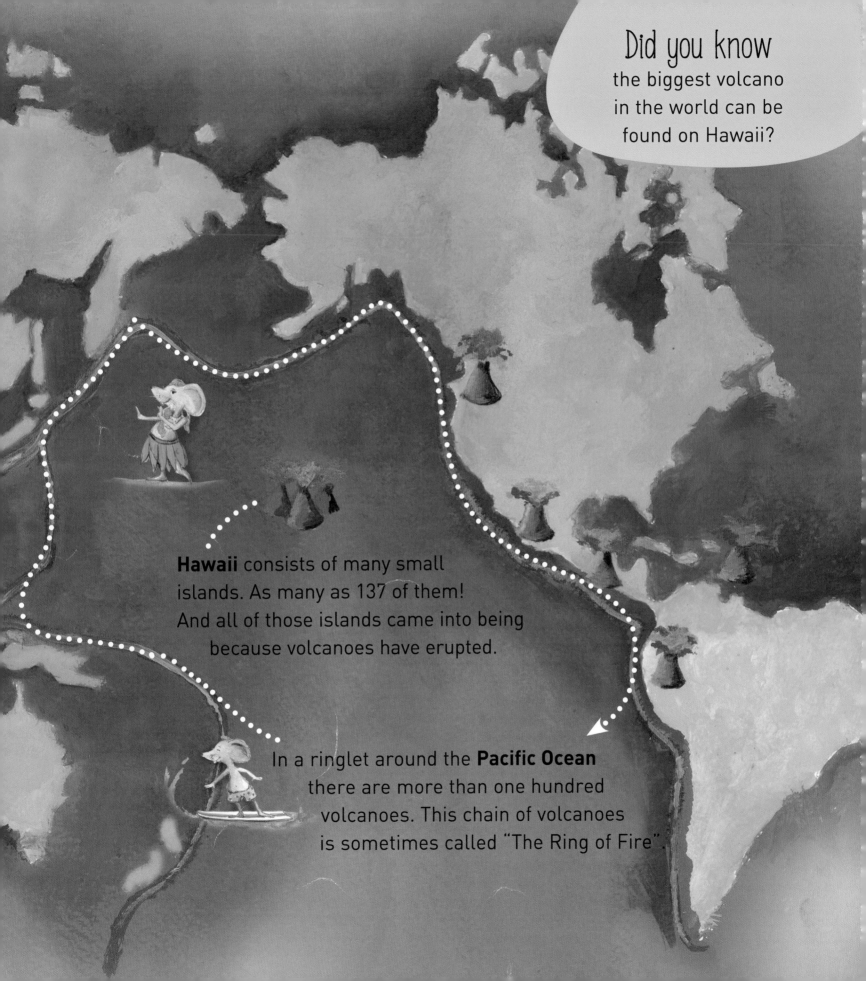

Did you know the biggest volcano in the world can be found on Hawaii?

Hawaii consists of many small islands. As many as 137 of them! And all of those islands came into being because volcanoes have erupted.

In a ringlet around the **Pacific Ocean** there are more than one hundred volcanoes. This chain of volcanoes is sometimes called "The Ring of Fire".

And here you can see what Mount Saint Helens looks like now. During the eruption a big chunk of the volcano collapsed: the tip disappeared and left a crater. Suddenly the mountain was about 1,300 feet smaller! A new mountaintop started growing right in the middle of that crater because it's an active volcano.

Kinds of volcanoes

There are various kinds of volcanoes.
If a volcano erupts every once in a while, it is called an **active volcano**. Volcanoes that have not erupted in a very long time are called **dormant volcanoes**. A dormant volcano could always wake up and start erupting again! An **extinct volcano** is a volcano that will probab never erupt again. The earth's crust has grown thick with rocks, so magma can no longer escape.

The active Fly Geyser in Nevada is famous because it did not come into being naturally. It was made by humans, by accident. People looking for water drilled a well in the ground, but a leak sprung in the well, and water has been escaping for years.

Usually volcanoes come into being very slowly. But the Paricutín, in Mexico, is famous because it grew so fast. It came into being in 1943 and it grew about 164 feet in just one day! Now the volcano is more than 1,300 feet tall. But luckily it has stopped growing. So now it is a dormant volcano, like Mount Saint Helens once was.

Living near a volcano

It is dangerous to live near a volcano. The lava that comes out during an eruption is like liquid fire. It burns everything on its way down the mountainside. The ash and steam that escape the volcano are also very dangerous. They can make it hard to breathe and make you sick.

Did you know

sometimes a cloud of volcanic ash can form above a volcano? This cloud is called an ash cloud. And when the volcanic ash falls down again, it is called ash rain.

Nevertheless some people live near dormant volcanoes because there are many benefits as well. The volcanic ash makes the soil fertile so farmers can grow fruits and vegetables. And the scenery is magnificent. Many people travel to see the landscape. That's why a lot of nice vacation destinations are near volcanoes.

Did you know scientists create power with the heat of volcanoes and geysers? So people who live in the area around a volcano can have free energy.

Volcanologists

There are some people who know a great deal about volcanoes. They study them and are called volcanologists. Because they keep a good eye on active volcanoes, volcanologists can sometimes predict when a volcano will erupt. Then they can warn people who live nearby to move to safety.

A **gasmask** is needed, because volcanoes release dangerous gases.

It is dangerous near volcanoes. That is why volcanologists often wear **helmets.**

Volcanologists never pick up solidified lava with their hands because it's way too hot to touch. They always use special **grabbers**.

To do their research, volcanologists have to collect lots of **stones and ash**.

Spitting Mad

I am so mad I could erupt
So angry I'm boiling
All the feelings must escape
I'm going to explode!

The earth rumbles
Steam comes out of my ears
I spit fire and ash
I roar and I pop

When I explode please let me be
Let me erupt like a volcano
Because hissing smoke makes me feel better
Breathing fire – just for a while – helps me cool down

Make your own volcano!

This is what you need:
a big flat plate
clay
a box of baking powder and some vinegar
red food coloring
a teaspoon and a little cup
and of course, a little bit of help from an adult

Preparation
1. Put some clay on the plate and make a nice
   mountain out of it. You can decide if you want
   your mountain to be tall or wide.
2. Use your fingers to create a hollow crater at the tip
   of the mountain. This is what you're going to use to
   turn your mountain into a volcano – it's from the
   crater the lava soon will be boiling!
3. Let the clay dry.

Erupting!
When the clay is dry, the real fun can begin!
You are ready to make your volcano erupt.

This is what you do:
1. Pour a dash of vinegar in a cup and
   add some red food coloring.
2. Stir well using the teaspoon.
3. Scatter the baking powder into the crater
   of the volcano.
4. Pour a little of the vinegar mixture over
   the baking powder.
5. Stir again.

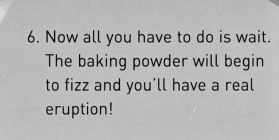

6. Now all you have to do is wait.
   The baking powder will begin
   to fizz and you'll have a real
   eruption!

Mini-quiz

1. What do we call molten rock when it's inside a volcano?

2. And what do we call molten rock when it escapes from the volcano?

3. What do we call the surface that covers the fiery center of the earth?

4. What's the name for a volcano that spouts water?

5. The earth's crust is made up of huge jigsaw pieces. Do volcanoes usually lie at the edges or at the center of those pieces?

6. Are most volcanoes on land or under water?

7. What do we call a volcano that erupts every once in a while?

8. And a volcano that hasn't erupted in a very long time?

9. What do we call the ash that falls down after a volcano erupts?

10. What do we call people who study volcanoes?

Answers

1. Magma

2. Lava

3. The earth's crust

4. A geyser

5. At the edges

6. Under water

7. An active volcano

8. A dormant volcano

9. Ash rain

10. Volcanologists

What a lovely things!

Do you know which ones are used by volcanologists?*

* Take a good look at the page about volcanologists.